LEGENDS OF WARFARE

NAVAL

USS Lexington (CV-2)

From the 1920s to the Battle of Coral Sea in WWII

DAVID DOYLE

SCHIFFER MILITARY

4880 Lower Valley Road   Atglen, PA 19310

Cover design by Justin Watkinson
Type set in Impact/Minion Pro/Univers LT Std

ISBN: 978-0-7643-6490-7
Printed in China

Published by Schiffer Publishing, Ltd.
4880 Lower Valley Road
Atglen, PA 19310
Phone: (610) 593-1777; Fax: (610) 593-2002
Email: Info@schifferbooks.com
Web: www.schifferbooks.com

For our complete selection of fine books on this and related subjects, please visit our website at www.schifferbooks.com. You may also write for a free catalog.

Schiffer Publishing's titles are available at special discounts for bulk purchases for sales promotions or premiums. Special editions, including personalized covers, corporate imprints, and excerpts, can be created in large quantities for special needs. For more information, contact the publisher.

We are always looking for people to write books on new and related subjects. If you have an idea for a book, please contact us at proposals@schifferbooks.com.

Acknowledgments

Warships, particularly capital ships, touch many lives. Their complexity, long service life, and considerable range bring them into contact with many more people than does, for example, a single tank or specific airplane. Accordingly, archival resources concerning USS *Lexington* were scattered from coast to coast and through the collections of a multitude of individuals and institutions, many which generously opened their resources for the creation of this book.

I would like to thank fellow authors Tom Kailbourn, Tom Laemlein, Robert C. Stern, A. D. Baker III, and Scott Taylor for their help with this project. Researchers Tracy White, Martin Quinn, Jerry Leslie, Roger Torgeson, Rick Davis, and Patty and James Noblin were very generous in sharing their discoveries with me. The archival resources of the National Archives at College Park, Maryland; San Bruno, California; and Seattle, Washington, yielded many treasures of information, as did the Hawaii State Archives, the National Museum of Naval Aviation, the San Diego Air and Space Museum, the Puget Sound Naval Shipyard, the US Naval Shipbuilding Museum, the Naval Historical Foundation, various branches of the National Park Service, and the US Army Museum of Hawaii. Robert Hanshew, Lisa Crunk, and Chuck Haberlein at the Naval History and Heritage Command were generous with their time and in providing access to the collection to complete this study.

My wonderful wife, Denise, scanned hundreds of images and sifted through thousands of pages of dusty documents, helping to pull together the materials presented here.

All photos not otherwise credited are from the collection of the US National Archives and Records Administration, College Park, Maryland.

Contents

Introduction

When the keel of USS *Lexington* was laid on the ways of the Fore River Ship and Engine Building Company, in Quincy, Massachusetts, on January 8, 1921, she was the lead ship of what was planned be the most powerful class of battle cruisers in the world. This new battle cruiser class, authorized by the Naval Act of 1916, was to include six ships: *Lexington*, *Constellation*, *Saratoga*, *Ranger*, *Constitution*, and *United States*. At the same time, six South Dakota–class battleships were ordered, and coupled with Lexington-class, battle cruisers would make the US Navy the most powerful fleet in the world. While these battleships were planned during 1919, forward-thinking US naval aviators were pushing for the construction of the Navy's first aircraft carrier. With the Navy's budget mostly consumed by the ambitious 1916 battleship and battle cruiser program, plans for a specialized aircraft carrier were put on hold.

Originally, each of the battle cruisers was to be armed with ten 14-inch, 50-caliber rifles. By the time construction began, their main armament had been changed to eight 16-inch, 50-caliber rifles. In terms of naval weaponry, the caliber of the gun is the barrel length divided by the bore; thus a 16-inch, 50-caliber gun is 800 inches long. At that time, battle cruiser designs created a heavily armed yet relatively lightly armored warship. These vessels relied on unusually high speed as a key element of their defense. USS *Lexington* was designed to steam at 35 knots, a pace unheard of at the time for such a large vessel. To achieve this speed meant a tremendous amount of power, in this case 180,000 horsepower, which was six times more powerful than the largest machinery the US Navy had built to that time—the 29,000 horsepower that drove USS *West Virginia* (BB-48). The *Lexington*-class battle cruisers were to displace 43,500 tons each, making them the heaviest ships in the fleet.

These ambitious projects were thrown into disarray with the signing of the Washington Naval Treaty on February 6, 1922. To promote international disarmament, and specifically to curtail Japan's rapid naval expansion, the treaty signatories were required to immediately suspend all capital ship construction. With the simple stroke of a pen, the Navy's battle cruiser plans were scuttled. However, the treaty did allow two existing capital ship hulls to be used as the basis for aircraft carriers. Their displacement was not to exceed 33,000 tons each (compared to the 27,000-ton limit otherwise imposed on carriers). In February 1922, *Lexington*, CC-1, was under construction at Fore River Shipyard in Quincy, Massachusetts, while *Saratoga*, CC-3, was being built by New York Shipbuilding in Camden, New Jersey. At this point, *Lexington* was 24.2 percent complete and *Saratoga* was 28 percent finished when their construction as battle cruisers was suspended. As the two battle cruisers closest to completion, *Lexington* and *Saratoga* were selected for conversion to aircraft carriers. The rest of the class, ranging from *Constellation* (22.7 percent complete) to *Ranger* (4 percent complete), were scrapped on the builders' ways.

Lexington was intended to be the lead ship of a class of battle cruisers named after her. This artist's conception depicts a Lexington-class battle cruiser. Two ships of the class, *Lexington* and *Saratoga*, were completed but converted to aircraft carriers.

Battle Cruiser *Lexington*, Proposed Specifications	
Displacement	43,500 long tons
Length	874 ft overall
Beam	105 feet, 4 inches
Draft	31 feet
Installed power	180,000 shp
Propulsion	four shafts, turboelectric drive
	16 water-tube boilers
Speed	33 knots (38 mph)
Range	10,000 nautical miles at 10 knots
Complement	1,297 (1,326 as flagship)
Armament	8 × 16-inch / .50-cal. guns in four two-gun turrets
	14 × 6-inch / 53-cal. in single mounts
	8 × 3-inch/ 50-cal. antiaircraft guns
	8 × 21-inch torpedo tubes, 4 submerged
Armored belt	5–7 inches
Barbette armor	5–9 inches
Deck armor	1.5–2.25 inches

CHAPTER 1

Prewar Years

At the same time, the Navy had been exploring various carrier designs and were hopeful that funds would soon be allocated for the project. One of the projected designs featured a displacement of 39,000 tons and a length of 850 feet, and the preliminary design was delivered on May 5, 1921. When the Washington Treaty was signed, it took only eleven days to adapt the 1921 carrier design to the *Lexington*-class hull. To meet treaty-imposed weight limitations, the new carrier design required greater refinement, and it took until December 21, 1923, before final plans were approved, and the shipyards were then instructed to proceed with the conversion of the two vessels. *Lexington* and *Saratoga* kept their original names, but their hull numbers changed to CV-2 and CV-3.

Haggling over the carrier weight limit delayed *Lexington*'s construction, but she was finally launched on October 3, 1925. *Lexington* was christened by Mrs. Theodore Douglas Robinson, whose husband was the assistant secretary of the Navy. Even though in the water, *Lexington* was far from being ready to put to sea. Tugs pushed her immense yet powerless hull along the Weymouth Fore River to the shipyard's fitting pier. She was moored there for the next two years as the workers transformed the battle cruiser hull into a state-of-the-art aircraft carrier. When completed, *Lexington* was commissioned on December 14, 1927, finally receiving the coveted "USS" before her name. Capt. Albert W. Marshall was placed in command that day, becoming the first of ten officers who would command *Lexington*.

After commissioning, *Lexington* moved to Charleston Navy Yard in South Boston on January 5, 1928, for final fitting out. En route, Capt. Marshall took her into Massachusetts Bay just long enough for a Vought UO-1 to land aboard. This was the first landing aboard a Lexington-class carrier, beating *Saratoga* (which was launched earlier) by about a week. After fitting out, *Lexington* set out on her shakedown cruise along the US East Coast. Then, *Lexington* sailed west through the Panama Canal, bound for the US West Coast. She would arrive in San Pedro on April 7, 1928, and be based there for the rest of her career.

The dramatic rise of the Japanese Empire in the years after World War I led many US policymakers to believe that the next major war would take place in the Pacific. To prepare for such a conflict, the Navy conducted numerous exercises in the Pacific Ocean during the interwar years. *Lexington* debuted in those exercises during a January 1929 scenario dubbed Fleet Problem IX. *Lexington* was assigned to Blue Force and was tasked with defending the Panama Canal from the Black Force, which included her sister ship, *Saratoga*. Prior to this exercise, USS *Langley*, the sole US carrier, had played only a minor role in scouting. During Fleet Problem IX, however, the judges determined that the mock attack by *Saratoga*'s aircraft had not only "destroyed" one end of the canal, but that each carrier's aircraft had "badly damaged" if not "sunk" the opposing force's carrier. The carriers would go on to play more-prominent roles in future exercises, and *Lexington* and *Saratoga* would face off against each other, as well as work together, in many fleet maneuvers until 1941.

During Fleet Problem IX, *Lexington* was commanded by Capt. Frank D. Berrien, who had relieved Capt. Albert Marshall on August 11, 1928. Capt. Berrien was, in turn, relieved on June 30, 1930, by Capt. Ernest King, who remained *Lexington*'s captain until May 31, 1932. Among those aboard *Lexington* during this time, there was a 1929 Annapolis graduate assigned to radio communications aboard the ship. Robert A. Heinlein would leverage his Navy experiences to become "the dean of science-fiction writers," with a focus on scientific accuracy in fiction writing.

Lexington was built at the Fore River Plant of Bethlehem Shipbuilding Corp. along the Weymouth Fore River at Quincy, Massachusetts. Originally designated CC-1, her keel was laid on January 8, 1921. In this March 29, 1921, photo, the keel and framing for the double bottom are in place amidships. Plates of the shell, the outer skin of the hull, have been installed on the frame, with some of the shell plates extending beyond the frame.

Original plans for *Lexington's* aircraft were to assign the planes as follows:

- two fighter (VF) squadrons consisting of eighteen operational and nine reserve aircraft each
- two torpedo (VT) squadrons comprising sixteen operational and eight reserve aircraft each
- a half squadron of observation aircraft (VO), consisting of twelve operational and six reserve aircraft
- three additional VO aircraft were assigned to a utility squadron

By the time *Lexington* joined the operational fleet, her squadron designations and assignments had been changed. When she steamed for Panama during Fleet Problem IX, she was carrying the following squadrons:

- VF-3B, flying Boeing F3B-1 fighters
- VT-1B, flying Martin T4M-1 torpedo bombers
- VB-1B, with a mixture of Curtiss F6C-2/3 and Boeing F3B-1 fighter aircraft
- VS-3B, flying Vought O2U-2 observation planes

The "B" suffix on the squadron numbers signified *Lexington's* assignment to the Battle Fleet.

In late 1929, *Lexington* would serve the United States in a unique way. At that time, the American Pacific Northwest was suffering through a drought, particularly Tacoma, Washington, a city that relied on hydroelectric power. Tacoma was drawing dangerously close to complete blackout conditions as the waters of the Nisqually and Skokomish Rivers dropped to a mere trickle. To save energy, Tacoma officials turned off the power to several of the city's largest businesses, and this had led to more than three hundred workers being laid off. Nearby Fort Lewis was also taking strong conservation measures, darkening the barracks at 1600 hours.

The massive turboelectric drives of *Lexington* and *Saratoga* had been widely touted in the press, and both the vessels were at Puget Sound Navy Yard, just 40 miles away. Tacoma officials appealed to President Herbert Hoover that one of the vessels sail to Tacoma and supply the city with power. A deal was made to have *Lexington* supply the city with electric power at a rate of one cent per kilowatt-hour. It took five days for Tacoma to construct 2 miles of high-tension power lines, stretching from the city dock to a power substation.

Lexington tied up at Tacoma's Baker Dock in Tacoma on December 15, 1929, and two days later current began to flow from her power plant to the beleaguered city. To supply the commercial 60-cycle current, *Lexington's* main turbine was run at 1,800 rpm, which was 45 rpm above the rated maximum. No apparent ill effects were experienced as *Lexington* remained in place supplying power until January 17, 1930, with the carrier providing 4,250,960 kilowatt-hours of energy to Tacoma. Shortly afterward, the city of Seattle, which had objected to *Lexington* servicing Tacoma, made a similar request for electric power, which the Navy declined.

Two months after serving as the city of Tacoma's emergency power plant, *Lexington* was steaming for the Caribbean and Fleet Problem X. *Lexington* was assigned to Black Force, the striking force, while *Saratoga* and *Langley* were part of the defending Blue Force.

By June 30, 1921, the keel and frame of the double bottom had been extended forward but not all the way to the bow. A lateral bulkhead has been erected at the forward end of the ship's vital machinery spaces; three temporary ladders are leaning against the top of the bulkhead. Staging, or scaffolding, rises on each side of the building ways; planks were laid higher and higher on the beams of the scaffolding as the sides of the hull took shape.

It would be five days into the exercise before contact was made by the Black and Blue teams, when *Lexington*'s aircraft found *Saratoga* and her task force. In the mock battle that followed, *Saratoga* and *Langley* were judged to be unable to sustain air operations. *Lexington*'s aircraft, on successive strikes, were also judged to have damaged other units in the Blue Force, including three battleships and a destroyer. One month later, during Fleet Problem XI, the roles of aggressor and defender were reversed, with *Lexington* protecting several islands in the Caribbean. This exercise indicated a strong need for additional scouting aircraft with better performance, including longer ranges and shorter takeoff spans.

On February 16, 1931, the Navy began Fleet Problem XII. *Lexington* and *Saratoga* formed part of the defending Blue Fleet, pitted against the bulk of the Navy's battleships augmented by the carrier *Langley*, as the Black force. The Black Fleet was tasked with capturing the Panama Canal as well as a hypothetical canal in Nicaragua. When the exercise ended in March, all three carriers passed through the Panama Canal on their way to more exercises off Cuba. On the last day of March, *Lexington*, under the command of Capt. King, was directed to assist Navy and Marine units with relief operations following a devastating earthquake, followed by a major fire in Managua, Nicaragua. This was the first time a US carrier provided aid during a natural disaster outside the US.

In a strange foreshadowing of future events, the joint Army-Navy "Grand Exercise 4," held during February 1932, showed that Hawaii could be successfully attacked by carriers. *Lexington* and *Saratoga*, under command of RAdm. Harry Yarnell, struck the Hawaiian Islands with a series of mock attacks that began on Sunday morning, February 7, with results that were judged as "very impressive" by the exercise umpires.

On November 3, 1933, the White House announced that the entire US fleet would visit the East Coast during 1934. A sailing date of April 9, 1934, was set, and on that day the 104 ships and 46,000 men under command of Adm. David Sellers put to sea, bound for the East Coast. En route to Panama, the force was divided into two mock fleets, and war games were conducted along the way, concluding with a simulated attack on the US Army defenders of the Panama Canal. Once the war games were concluded, it took forty-seven hours for the armada to pass through the Panama Canal. Once in the Caribbean, additional fleet exercises took place. In the early morning of May 31, the fleet arrived off New York City, to find the Big Apple surrounded by fog.

As the fog lifted and the sun was bright in the sky, the fleet formed a column and passed before President Franklin D. Roosevelt, who reviewed the might of the US Navy from the cruiser *Indianapolis* (CA-35). Adm. Sellers led the fleet aboard the flagship, the battleship *Pennsylvania* (BB-38). *Pennsylvania* was followed by *Saratoga*, with her two destroyer plane guards, and then *Lexington* and her plane guards. After passing *Indianapolis*, *Saratoga* and *Lexington* turned into the wind and launched a combined 185 aircraft. Once the air operations were complete, both carriers tied up to Pier 90 in New York City. They would remain there, open to the public for tours, until June 19.

During the summer of 1935, *Lexington* entered Puget Sound Navy Yard for a major refitting, the work focused primarily on her antiaircraft (AA) defenses. When *Lexington* entered the Navy Yard for the refit, her antiaircraft battery was a meager .50-caliber machine

The progress of construction of *Lexington* is viewed from off the starboard stern in a October 1, 1921, photograph. The space enclosed by the first two lateral bulkheads will be the location of the main driving motors for the two inboard propellers. Immediately forward of this space, toward the center will be ammunition magazines and handling rooms, while on each side will be the main driving motors for the outboard propellers.

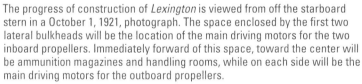

Lexington is viewed from amidships toward the bow on February 14, 1922. Snow blankets the deck plates in the foreground, while the beams that will support the deck as it is extended forward are visible in the background. During the month this photo was taken, construction on *Lexington* was suspended under the strictures of the Washington Naval Treaty; the ship was 24.2 percent complete.

gun atop each of the super-firing 8-inch turrets. Consequently, *Lexington*'s armament was augmented by a machine gun platform encircling the funnel at the fifth level, with six .50-caliber machine guns mounted on the port side of the funnel, and a like number of AA machine guns mounted to starboard. The machine guns atop the 8-inch turrets were removed, while machine gun platforms were added on either side of the flight deck near the ends. Each of these platforms could accommodate up to four of the heavy Browning M2 water-cooled AA machine guns.

The next year, *Lexington* returned to Puget Sound for further, even more noticeable, alterations. The forward portion of the flight deck was substantially widened, on the basis of the rationale that with the ship's turboelectric drive and hull design, *Lexington* could make essentially the same speed both ahead and astern. Aircraft are normally launched over the bow and recovered over the stern, using the airflow over the ship to aid the aircraft's lift. Widening the flight deck forward and installing additional arrestor gear would allow *Lexington* to recover aircraft over the bow while backing at full speed, which could be a significant advantage in the event of emergency.

Further modernization was planned for *Lexington* and her sister ship, *Saratoga*, and Congress appropriated $15 million for the work during June 1939. However, with the outbreak of war in Europe the Navy was unwilling to sideline its two largest carriers for a projected eleven months, and the work was postponed.

The shape of *Lexington* as viewed off her port bow is visible behind the staging and crane supports in a March 1, 1922, photo. Unlike her sister ship, *Saratoga*, which was built under a massive shed at Camden, New Jersey, *Lexington* was built out in the open.

Rather than scrap *Lexington* and *Saratoga* under terms of the Washington Naval Treaty, the Navy drafted plans to convert them to aircraft carriers. In March 1922, a panel of admirals used models to explain the conversion to the House Naval Affairs Committee. *National Museum of Naval Aviation*

The barbettes for the four twin 16-inch turrets of *Lexington* are under construction on March 1, 1922. If the ship had been completed as a battle cruiser, the barbettes would have held operating machinery and ammunition-handling spaces below the turrets.

On July 1, 1922, authorization was approved to complete *Lexington* and *Saratoga* as aircraft carriers. This photo, dated October 3, 1922, showing the progress of construction on "Airplane Carrier No. 2," as *Lexington* had been redesignated, was taken from over the forward part of the hull, facing aft. One of the lower decks is taking shape, with some plates having been laid down amidships. The plates were predrilled for rivets.

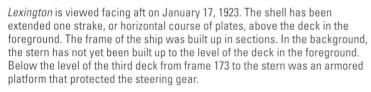

Lexington is viewed facing aft on January 17, 1923. The shell has been extended one strake, or horizontal course of plates, above the deck in the foreground. The frame of the ship was built up in sections. In the background, the stern has not yet been built up to the level of the deck in the foreground. Below the level of the third deck from frame 173 to the stern was an armored platform that protected the steering gear.

The area of the ship in the background of the preceding photo is viewed close-up on January 17, 1923. On the Lexington-class carriers, the third deck (i.e., the third full deck below the flight deck) was the armored deck, comprising a layer of 50-pound STS (special treatment steel) over one of 30-pound STS, yielding a thickness of 2 inches.

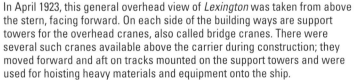

In April 1923, this general overhead view of *Lexington* was taken from above the stern, facing forward. On each side of the building ways are support towers for the overhead cranes, also called bridge cranes. There were several such cranes available above the carrier during construction; they moved forward and aft on tracks mounted on the support towers and were used for hoisting heavy materials and equipment onto the ship.

The photographer was positioned over frame 193 well aft on *Lexington*, probably poised on an overhead crane, when he took this photo facing forward to document the state of construction on July 12, 1923. Farther forward, amidships, work is underway on a transverse bulkhead and some of the compartments on the outboard sides of the deck. In the background toward the bow, much of the plating of this deck remains to be installed.

This elevated view of *Lexington* was taken from above frame 104, facing aft, on January 24, 1924. At the center of the photo, work has begun on a deck, apparently the main deck, with the structure of the aft elevator well taking shape on that piece of deck. To the right, the indentation in the deck with the curve at its aft end is the floor and lower part of a boat pocket, one of four such pockets built into the port side of the hull to house boats.

Work on the hangar deck, or second deck, is documented in an April 11, 1924, photo taken above frame 104, facing forward. Much of the hangar deck would be occupied by hangar space, where spare aircraft and those requiring maintenance would be housed. This deck would also hold crew quarters, the laundry, stowage spaces, vegetable lockers, ventilation ducts, the boiler uptakes, CPO mess rooms, the sick bay, and other compartments.

In a view taken above frame 82, facing toward the bow, on October 14, 1924, in the foreground is the partially completed flight deck and the forward elevator well, which would be T-shaped once the flight deck was extended forward of the well.

In another October 14, 1924, photo, *Lexington* is viewed from above frame 133, facing forward. The uppermost deck is the flight deck, and it is pierced by the rectangular aft elevator well. Below the flight deck are the uncompleted main deck and the hangar deck.

Taken on the same date as the preceding two photos is this view from above frame 67, looking aft, with the forward elevator well occupying the forward part of the built-up structure in the foreground. The aft elevator well is visible in the distance.

As seen facing aft from frame 127 on January 15, 1925, the aft part of the hull of *Lexington* was slowly being built upward after the amidships area already had been built as far upward as the flight deck. Compartments are under construction to the sides.

The flight deck of *Lexington* is observed from frame 130 forward on April 23, 1925. The aft elevator well is in the foreground. The four rectangular openings in the flight deck to the right are boiler uptakes, which will be routed up through the smokestack.

Also taken on April 23, 1925, this view shows the flight deck, facing forward, from frame 92. Work on the flight deck had proceeded only to the front of the forward elevator; forward of that point, work continues on the lower decks toward the bow.

The rudder of *Lexington* is seen from the starboard side on April 23, 1925. Several scaffold planks are set up next to the front edge of the rudder. Also in view above the scaffolding to the right is the starboard inboard propeller bracket, or propeller strut.

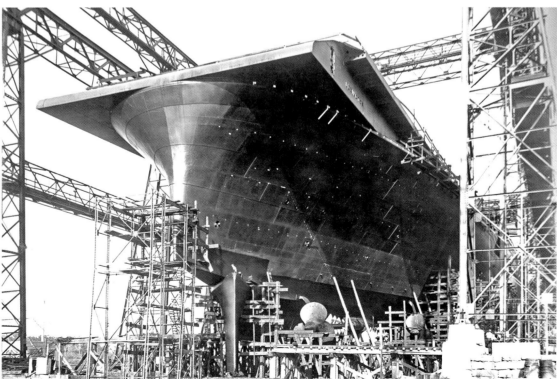

By July 10, 1925, the propellers and propeller shafts had been fitted to *Lexington*. The rudder is turned hard to starboard. The design of the stern is also displayed. The rear of the ramp at the aft end of the flight deck came even with the top of the stern.

Lexington was photographed on the building ways at Fore River on October 2, 1925, the day before her launching. Scaffolding has been cleared from the area, leaving only the overhead cranes and their support towers standing. Light-colored poppets attached to the bottom of the hull will stabilize and protect the narrow forward part of the hull during launching. On the upper part of the side of the hull, the forward gun gallery and the four boat pockets are visible.

On the day before her launching, a photographer on an overhead crane took this view of the forward part of the flight deck, with the forward elevator at the bottom of the photo. The round opening in the deck to the right is for mounting the forward 8-inch gun turret.

The forward elevator well, fitted with scaffolding and a temporary bulkhead, is viewed from starboard on October 2, 1925. The elevator would occupy the front part of the well, while the aft part would have two downward-folding panels at flight-deck level.

The flight deck of *Lexington* is viewed from frame 65, facing aft, on October 2, 1925. The T shape of the forward elevator is apparent; the aft extension of the T was to accommodate extra-long aircraft. Temporary safety rails are on the edges of the deck.

This view of the aft elevator taken the day before launching bears the original inscription, "Elevator opening for bringing small parts from hangar deck." In time, the aft elevator would prove to be of limited use because of its small size, and both elevators were slow.

On October 2, 1925, with one day left to go before the launching of *Lexington*, crews are applying shoring to immobilize the rudder and the propellers during the launching. Light-colored poppets are fitted underneath the hull, secured with fittings farther up on the sides of the hull. After launching, the poppets were removed. Written on the hull above the propellers, for the benefit of the tugboat crews who will assist *Lexington* once launched, is "WHEEL / KEEP CLEAR."

The stern of *Lexington* is portrayed on the day before launching, also showing the ramp at the aft end of the flight deck. The assembly attached to the upper edge of the rudder is shoring, designed to immobilize the rudder during the stern-first launching.

The rudder and its temporary shoring are observed from the port side on October 2, 1925. Painted in white are draft marks, indicating the distance from the keel to the waterline in feet. As built, *Lexington* had a minimum draft of 24.25 feet and a maximum of 30.5 feet.

The day before the launching, *Lexington* sits poised on the ways. At the bow are three hawsepipes for three anchors. The bulbous bow was designed to optimize the flow of water around the bow and the hull, reducing drag and improving performance.

Old Glory affixed to her bow, *Lexington* slides down the ways on October 3, 1925. The ship was sponsored by Mrs. Theodore D. Robinson, the wife of the assistant secretary of the Navy. A number of people are on the flight deck for the launching. *National Museum of Naval Aviation*

Lexington is now fully in the water upon launching, still moving rearward under the momentum of her slide into the Weymouth Fore River. With much construction left to be finished on the ship, she is riding high on the water, allowing a view of much of her armored belt. Located above and below the waterline adjacent to the vital machinery spaces within the ship, the armored belt was about 9 feet, 4 inches high, with a width of 7 inches from the top down 3 feet, and from there tapering to 5 inches in thickness at the bottom. *US Naval Shipbuilding Museum*

Tugboats line up alongside *Lexington* after her launching. Since *Lexington* was unable to navigate under her own power at that point, tugboats were required to move the ship to her fitting-out dock at the Fore River Plant, where work would continue on her. *National Museum of Naval Aviation*

The flight deck of *Lexington* is in view immediately after the launching. The openings for the forward and aft elevators are visible on the flight deck. The main-battery turrets, the superstructure or island, the smokestack, and other fixtures were yet to be installed.

Lexington moves toward her fitting-out dock at the Fore River Plant on October 3, 1925. To the right is the Argentinian battleship *Rivadavia*, built at Fore River from 1910 to 1915. At the time of *Lexington's* launching, she was undergoing modernization there.

Civilian spectators look on and passengers line the rails on the flight deck as *Lexington* continues her short journey from building ways to fitting-out dock. Toward the top of the hull, the cutout for the yet-to-be-constructed forward starboard gun gallery is visible.

Lexington rests at her fitting-out dock at Fore River on January 13, 1926. Scaffolding is erected on a barge adjacent to the bow, and the gun gallery is under construction, with scaffolding erected below it. Scaffolding is also suspended on the bow below the front edge of the flight deck. To the right is *AB-1*, a crane ship that was converted from the battleship USS *Kearsarge* (BB-5). It supplemented the fixed cranes on the opposite side of *Lexington*.

The aft port side of *Lexington* is observed at the fitting-out dock at Fore River on January 13, 1926. Two of the four boat pockets on the port side are visible. Recessed in the hull along the main deck level just below the flight deck is the aft port gun gallery.

The flight deck of *Lexington* is viewed from frame 120, facing aft, on January 15, 1926. The frame number, mentioned often in this book, refers to the transverse frames of the ship, numbered consecutively, forward to aft. The frame number was often used to refer to a specific longitudinal point on the ship. To the left are several of the boiler uptakes, fitted with temporary covers and with guardrails surrounding them. To the right is *AB-1*.

In an April 10, 1926, photograph of *Lexington's* main deck, facing forward, to the right are the boiler uptakes, which will later be extended up through the smokestack. In the background on the starboard side, construction of the superstructure has begun.

The flight deck of *Lexington* is viewed facing aft from a position adjacent to where the front of the smokestack eventually would be. To the left are the uptakes, and just aft of the one to the rear, construction of the smokestack has just started. At the center of the deck, adjacent to the rear of the smokestack, is the aft elevator well, covered with a tarp. Some of the wooden decking has been applied to the steel flight deck.

The smokestack is taking shape to the left in this view of the flight deck of *Lexington*, looking aft, on July 7, 1926. Above the flight deck, the uptakes are routed into four smoke pipes, housed inside the smokestack. Thus, there would be four outlets to the smoke pipes atop the smokestack when it was completed. At the bottom of the photo is part of the forward elevator well; a section of deck is also open aft of the well.

The forward elevator well is viewed from above, facing forward, in another July 7, 1926, photograph. The section of deck that has not yet been installed to the rear of the well is visible. Large components were still being lowered belowdecks for installation, which may account for the gap in the flight deck aft of the elevator well. To the right, scaffolding encloses the superstructure, which is under construction.

Machinery (as built)

Total weight	6,894 tons
Boilers	16 Yarrow; 295 psi, 522 degrees F.
Propulsion turbogenerators	General Electric, 13 stage, 3 phase, 35,200 kW, 4,980 volts
Drive motors	General Electric, squirrel cage, rotor wound, 5,000 volts, two per shaft
Shaft horsepower	212,702 during trial; 180,000 design
Maximum speed	34.99 knots trial; 33.25 knots design
Lighting / ship's service power plant	6 General Electric 750 kW turbo generators
Emergency lighting, prior to 1942	batteries
Endurance	10 knots, 10,950 miles
Fuel	2,637 tons oil

Lexington had four twin 8-inch/55-caliber Mk. 9 Mod. 1 gun mounts, two forward of the superstructure and two aft of the smokestack. Seen here on July 7, 1926, are the two aft mounts, trained inboard, with the smokestack under construction just forward of them.

Staging for workmen fitting out Lexington surrounds the smokestack and superstructure and is hanging from the port side of the hull in a photograph taken at Fore River on October 7, 1926. The pilothouse is under construction atop the superstructure.

The photographer apparently gained access to the top of the smokestack to take this view of *Lexington*, facing forward, on October 7, 1926. To the right, the tripod-shaped foremast is under construction. Forward of the lower part of the mast is the pilothouse, its top open pending the addition of the next level of the superstructure. To the left is the forward elevator well. The flap doors have been installed at the rear extension of the well; when raised, the flaps formed part of the flight deck, and when lowered, they provided clearance for extra-large aircraft.

A view of *Lexington* at the fitting-out dock at Fore River shows much of her port side on January 4, 1927. Forward fire-control platforms have been installed on the foremast, and the bipod-type stub mainmast with the aft fire-control towers is aft of the smokestack.

By the time this photo was taken on April 7, 1927, the bridge had been installed around the pilothouse. The main-battery director top is above the pilothouse, mounted on the foremast, and at the top of the foremast, the secondary-battery control top is being built.

Lexington is viewed off her port bow at Fore River on April 7, 1927. At this point in time, the carrier had eight months more of fitting-out work to be completed before she would be commissioned. The compartment partway up the front of the smokestack is the secondary conning station, where the ship could be controlled if the pilothouse was disabled, on top of which is the open-topped primary aviation control station, or Pri-Fly.

The smokestack and the two aft 8-inch gun turrets are viewed facing forward on July 8, 1927. Work is still underway on the aft main-battery and secondary-battery control stations on the stub mainmast aft of the smokestack. The turrets had three doors per side.

In the interim since the similar photograph of *Lexington* was taken on April 7, 1927, in this July 8, 1927, photo the top of the foremast has been installed and scaffolding has been removed from the side of the smokestack. Three months remain until commissioning.

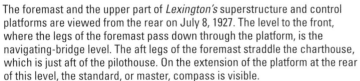

The foremast and the upper part of *Lexington's* superstructure and control platforms are viewed from the rear on July 8, 1927. The level to the front, where the legs of the foremast pass down through the platform, is the navigating-bridge level. The aft legs of the foremast straddle the charthouse, which is just aft of the pilothouse. On the extension of the platform at the rear of this level, the standard, or master, compass is visible.

On October 4, 1927, fitting-out of *Lexington* is advancing. The boom of the aircraft crane is propped up on blocks in the left foreground. Situated on top of the pilothouse is the 20-foot rangefinder. A substantial amount of ship's rigging has been installed.

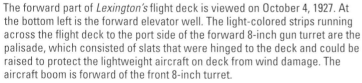

The forward part of *Lexington's* flight deck is viewed on October 4, 1927. At the bottom left is the forward elevator well. The light-colored strips running across the flight deck to the port side of the forward 8-inch gun turret are the palisade, which consisted of slats that were hinged to the deck and could be raised to protect the lightweight aircraft on deck from wind damage. The aircraft boom is forward of the front 8-inch turret.

The smokestack of *Lexington* is viewed from the front in an October 4, 1927, photograph. Midway up the front of the stack is the secondary conning station, an enclosed compartment with large windows. Directly above this station is the primary aviation control station, Pri-Fly. This station was where air operations on the carrier were controlled under the supervision of the air officer. It was open topped for better visibility.

An aerial view portrays *Lexington* on October 13, 1927. The exterior of the ship had been painted between early July and early October in a scheme of Navy Gray, with the flight deck stained in a mahogany or maroon color and steel decks painted Dark Gray.

Lexington, center, is viewed from the front in another October 13, 1927, aerial view. The contrast of the stained flight deck with the Navy Gray steel structures is apparent. Today, the heavy cruiser USS *Salem* (CA-139) is on permanent display in this part of the yard.

Appearing in a nearly pristine Navy Gray paint scheme, *Lexington* rests dockside at the Fore River Shipyard around the time of her December 1927 commissioning. All three anchors are now present, including one on each side of the bow and one on the centerline of the bow. Above the anchors are two hawseholes for mooring lines. The snubbed-off shape of the forward end of the flight deck is apparent. Life nets are rigged along the edges of the flight deck. *San Diego Air and Space Museum*

This view of part of *Lexington's* port side shows all four boat pockets on that side of the ship. A key difference between *Lexington* and her sister ship, *Saratoga*, was that Sara had a catwalk halfway up each side of the smokestack, while *Lexington* did not. *San Diego Air and Space Museum*

Lexington's port amidships is viewed close-up toward the end of her fitting-out period. A good view is provided of one of the boat pockets. The structure on the bottom of the 8-inch gun control compartment above the pilothouse is the radio-compass booth. *San Diego Air and Space Museum*

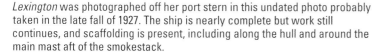

Lexington was photographed off her port stern in this undated photo probably taken in the late fall of 1927. The ship is nearly complete but work still continues, and scaffolding is present, including along the hull and around the main mast aft of the smokestack.

Lexington is viewed from a lower angle toward the end of her fitting-out period. On the port side of the hull, boat booms are in their stowed positions. On the stern are three booms for rigging a life net. Several ventilation doors are open on the stern. *Boston Public Library*

At the conclusion of the fitting-out period at Fore River Shipyard, officers and crew are assembled on the flight deck of *Lexington* for her commissioning ceremony. The ship now was entitled to bear the designation USS, United States Ship, before her name. *San Diego Air and Space Museum*

The US flag is hoisted on the aft end of USS *Lexington's* flight deck during the commissioning ceremony, December 14, 1927. When all of the ship's flags were hoisted simultaneously during the ceremony, it marked the formal commissioning of the ship.

USS *Lexington* rests at the fitting-out dock at Fore River Shipyard, Quincy, Massachusetts, at around the time of her December 1927 commissioning. In this view, the outline of the top of the ship's armored belt is visible amidships above the waterline. By now, the 5-inch/25-caliber Mk. 10 Mod. 1 gun mounts had been installed on the four galleries just below the flight deck; three gun mounts were on each gallery, with two galleries on each side of the ship. *National Museum of Naval Aviation*

A photograph taken from one of the forward fire-control tops of *Lexington* on December 20, 1927, documents the appearance of the forward part of the flight deck six days after her December 14 commissioning. The palisade has been erected on the deck to the port side of the forward 8-inch gun turret. A round platform with safety rails for a machine gun mount is on the roof of the second 8-inch turret. Toward the front of the flight deck are catapult tracks for launching seaplanes.

The smokestack and mid-to-aft part of the flight deck of *Lexington* are the subjects of this December 20, 1927, photograph taken from one of the forward fire-control tops. Toward the bottom is a platform with four 6-pounder saluting guns. Farther up on the front of the smokestack is the secondary conning station and Pri-Fly. A plank for a workman is suspended over the side of the secondary conning station. In the background, the aft elevator well is visible. Life nets are erected around the flight deck.

Tugboats assist USS *Lexington* as she leaves the fitting-out area at Fore River Shipyard on January 5, 1928. In the background is the Washington Street swing bridge, standing open to admit the carrier. A boat is visible in each of the three boat pockets seen here.

Lexington slips by the Washington Street swing bridge as she departs the Fore River Shipyard on January 5, 1928. From this angle, it can be seen that the secondary conning station on the front of the smokestack was not entirely enclosed but was open at the rear. *National Museum of Naval Aviation*

Moments after the preceding photo was taken, *Lexington* has cleared the swing bridge and is ready to navigate the series of bays between Quincy and her next destination, drydock at the South Boston Navy Yard Annex, where her lower hull will be painted. *National Museum of Naval Aviation*

A tradition in the US Navy is for newly commissioned ships to receive a silver service. Civic officials of Lexington, Massachusetts, presented USS *Lexington* with her set when the carrier was in drydock at South Boston Navy Yard Annex in early 1928. *San Diego Air and Space Museum*

Lexington enters drydock number 3 at South Boston Navy Yard Annex on January 11, 1928. Numbers of hawsers running from the ship are secured to the dock in order to position the ship in the proper place before the water is pumped out of the drydock.

The aft end of *Lexington* is viewed in drydock 3, caisson gate to the right, on January 11, 1928. The three booms on the stern for rigging a life net are prominent. A flagstaff was erected on the ramp at the aft end of the flight deck when the ship visited a port.

Lexington is viewed from an elevated position, probably on the movable crane seen in the preceding photo, as the ship is positioned in drydock 3 at South Boston Navy Yard Annex. The catapult tracks for launching seaplanes are visible on the flight deck.

As water is pumped out of drydock 3 on January 11, 1928, men in boats scrape marine growth that has accumulated below the waterline on the hull of *Lexington*. The object was to remove marine growth quickly, since it would harden once exposed to air. *National Museum of Naval Aviation*

All of the water has been extracted from the drydock on January 11, 1928. Keel blocks below the ship's keel and bilge blocks at intervals to the sides of the keel supported the ship in drydock, allowing painters and workmen to access the underside of the hull. *Boston Public Library*

Drydock 3 at the South Boston Navy Yard Annex is almost free of water. A close examination of the photograph reveals that aft of the bow there are still workmen on boats at the turn of the hull. A good view is also provided of the bulbous bow. *Boston Public Library*

As *Lexington* is prepared for postcommissioning work on her lower hull at drydock 3 at the South Boston Annex, several men visible at the lower left of the photo—apparently photographers—pack up their tripods. Drydock 3 was one of the largest drydocks on the East Coast. *Boston Public Library*

Workmen on the floor of the drydock near the bow are scraping the hull and apparently assessing the work to be done. In the background at the bottom of the hull is the curved shape of the port bilge keel, meant to counteract the ship's tendency to roll.

The stern of *Lexington* is viewed in drydock 3 at the South Boston Annex. Staging has been erected to give workmen access to all four propellers. On the stern above the hinge points at the bottoms of the three life-net booms are ventilator doors, shown in the closed positions. Hanging from the undersides of the aft part of the flight deck are four kedge anchors, two per side. These were used to prevent the ship from swinging around the forward anchor. *San Diego Air and Space Museum*

The port side of the rudder and the port inboard propeller of *Lexington* are in view in this photo taken during the ship's drydocking in early January 1929. When a US Navy ship was drydocked, it was routine to inspect the propellers and check their pitch.

The two port propellers of *Lexington* are shown while the ship is drydocked on January 11, 1928. Also in view are the propeller brackets or struts and propeller shafts. Underneath the keel, the keel blocks that supported the weight of the ship are visible.

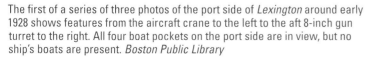

The first of a series of three photos of the port side of *Lexington* around early 1928 shows features from the aircraft crane to the left to the aft 8-inch gun turret to the right. All four boat pockets on the port side are in view, but no ship's boats are present. *Boston Public Library*

After *Lexington* completed her time in drydock at the South Boston Annex in early 1928, she began receiving her aircraft. Parked just aft of the aft elevator on *Lexington* is a Martin T3M torpedo bomber with markings for Torpedo Squadron 1B (VT-1B).

Details of the designs of the port side of the island, foremast, forward and aft fire-control tops, smokestack, and aft 8-inch turrets are visible. The interior of the aft elevator well is painted white, contrasting with the mahogany or maroon stain on the flight deck. *Boston Public Library*

During her shakedown cruise in early 1928, *Lexington* stopped in Newport, Rhode Island, to take on equipment and ordnance, including torpedoes for her torpedo bombers. Here, crewmen ease a torpedo down onto a trolley on the flight deck of *Lexington*. *San Diego Air and Space Museum*

In early 1928, civilians look over planes of *Lexington's* air group, apparently on a dock preparatory to embarking on the carrier. To the right is Curtiss F6C-3 Hawk Bureau Number (BuNo) A-7153, side number 5-F-16, of Fighting Squadron 5A (VF-5A). *San Diego Air and Space Museum*

Crewmen push a torpedo from one of *Lexington's* elevators onto a deck. The warhead is not installed. As built, the ship had two torpedo workshops and storage compartments, located on the main deck and the upper half deck just forward of the forward elevator. *San Diego Air and Space Museum*

During early 1928, sailors remove snow from the flight deck of *Lexington*. The man to the right is holding a shovel marked "V-2," indicating it was the property of the V-2 division, which was responsible for aircraft-handling operations on the hangar deck. *San Diego Air and Space Museum*

Crewmen shovel snow from the forward part of *Lexington's* flight deck. Stretching across the deck adjacent to the forward 8-inch turret is the raised palisade, with several of its slats left lowered to provide a passageway for deck crewmen through the palisade. *Boston Public Library*

On the flagstaff at the aft end of the flight deck of USS *Lexington* around early 1928, a chaplain's pennant flies above the United States flag. The chaplain's pennant was flown above the flag of the United States during church services for naval personnel conducted aboard a US Navy ship. The chaplain's pennant was white with a dark-blue Latin cross oriented sideways. It was the only flag or pennant that could be flown above the US flag. *Boston Public Library*

USS *Lexington* General Data

Dimensions

Length, overall, as built	888 feet, 6 inches
Length between perpendiculars	850 feet
Maximum beam	130 feet, 1½ inch
Waterline beam, as built	105 feet, 5¼ inches
Waterline beam, post-1936	111 feet, 9 inches
Flight deck dimensions, 1941	866 feet, 2 inches × 105 feet, 11¼ inches
Hangar deck	393 feet × 68 feet × 20 feet
Draft, max, as built	31 feet, 10⅜ inches
Displacement, light	34,067 tons
Displacement, standard	41,187 tons
Displacement, full load, 1936	43,054 tons
Displacement, full load, 1942	47,879 tons
Aviation fuel	137,450 gallons

Armor

Main belt	5 to 7 inches
Flight and hangar deck	0 inches
Protective deck	2 inches
Conning tower	80 lb. STS
Ship's complement, as designed	148 officers, 1,500 men
Ship's complement, 1938	79 officers, 1,354 men
Ship's complement, 1941	82 officers, 1509 men
Air wing, 1941	197 officers, 664 enlisted

Armament

1927	8 × 8 inch / 55 cal.; 12 × 5 inch / 25 cal.
1941	8 × 8 inch / 55 cal.; 12 × 5 inch / 25 cal.; 5 × 3 inch / 50 cal.; 8 × .50 cal. BMG
1942	12 × 5 inch / 25 cal.; 12 × 1.1-inch / 75 cal. quad mounts; 22 × 20 mm; 20 × .50 cal. BMG

Tugboats assist *Lexington* to maneuver into position in Boston Harbor around early 1928. The weather is chilly, judging by the blue coats the sailors on deck are wearing. On the side of the ship at the main-deck level, above the smokestack of the second tugboat from the right, the ship's name is spelled out. The name *Lexington* also was on the corresponding location on the opposite side of the ship.

In a scene possibly taken on the same occasion as the preceding photograph, tugboats crowd around *Lexington*, helping her move into position. It is possible that a censor airbrushed this photo to hide certain details, such as the aft elevator, since much of the flight deck is devoid of details, whereas other details are clearly visible. When *Lexington* entered service, the Navy discouraged the taking of aerial views of her. *San Diego Air and Space Museum*

Another photo, probably taken at Boston Harbor in early 1928, shows *Lexington* being assisted by tugboats. On the edge of the gun gallery on the main-deck level above the forwardmost tugboat are three semicircular platform extensions in the stowed positions.

Unlike *Saratoga*, which had a catwalk midway up each side of the smokestack, *Lexington* had a catwalk on the starboard side only, as seen in this photo. Farther up on the side of the smokestack are two searchlight platforms, accessible by ladders from the catwalk.

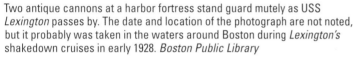

Two antique cannons at a harbor fortress stand guard mutely as USS *Lexington* passes by. The date and location of the photograph are not noted, but it probably was taken in the waters around Boston during *Lexington's* shakedown cruises in early 1928. *Boston Public Library*

In a companion piece to the preceding photo, three tugboats accompany *Lexington* in a harbor on a wintry day. Forward of the boat pocket on the starboard side of the hull were twenty-eight ventilator doors; although it is clearly a frigid day, many of those doors are open. *Boston Public Library*

Lexington's bow pointing into the wind, a biplane takes off from the flight deck. The first flight from *Lexington* occurred on January 5, 1928, during the carrier's trip from Fore River to South Boston Annex, when Mel Pride flew a Vought OU-1 off the ship. *San Diego Air and Space Museum*

As an aircraft comes in for a landing on *Lexington*, the two types of arrestor wires the ship originally was fitted with are visible: lateral wires, which the plane tried to grab with its arrestor hook, and longitudinal wires supported by "fiddle bridge" supports. *San Diego Air and Space Museum*

A view of the hangar deck in 1928 gives a sense of the dimensions of the massive hangar several decks below the main deck. Compartments on each side of the deck limited the width of the hangar. Parked on the forward part of the hangar deck are F6C-3s of VF-5. *National Museum of Naval Aviation*

Wings folded, two Martin T3M-2 torpedo bombers of Torpedo Squadron 1B (VT-1B) are parked on the hangar deck of USS *Lexington*. The T3M-2 to the right is BuNo A-7236. The T3M-2 was equipped with the 770-horsepower Packard 3A-2500 inline engine. *San Diego Air and Space Museum*

In 1928, Martin T4M-1s of Torpedo Squadron 1 (VT-1) are being spotted in place on the flight deck of *Lexington* while another T4M-1 with wings folded is being brought up on an elevator. The T4M-1 was similar to the T3M, except with a radial engine.

Aircraft are lined up on the flight deck of *Lexington* around 1928 as sailors and officers dressed in whites stand by. Several of the planes have markings for VF-3B on top of their wings. The planes in the foreground exhibit aileron locks on the lower wings. *National Museum of Naval Aviation*

In January 1928, *Lexington*, originally slated to become flagship of the Scouting Fleet in the Atlantic, was ordered to join the Battle Fleet, based at Long Beach, California. The voyage included a transit of the Panama Canal, as seen here on March 25, 1928.

Sailors in *Lexington's* forward port 5-inch/25-caliber gun gallery watch the proceedings during the transit of the Gatun Locks on March 25, 1928. The guns are at maximum elevation. The locks could barely accommodate the ship, with mere feet to spare on each side. *National Museum of Naval Aviation*

Lexington navigates through a cut in the Panama Canal in late March 1928. The photograph was taken from the port wing of the forward secondary, or 5-inch, control station atop the foremast, facing aft. Protruding from the smokestack is the range light. *National Museum of Naval Aviation*

Sailors dressed in whites line the rails as *Lexington* prepares to enter the Pedro Miguel Locks of the Panama Canal. Two small boats are stowed on the flight deck, and to the right of center on the forward part of the deck, the tracks of the catapult are visible.

It is a tight squeeze as *Lexington* negotiates the Miraflores Locks of the Panama Canal on March 25, 1928. Visible to the front of the two boats on the flight deck in this photo and the preceding one is a removable mast that held at its top the masthead light.

The stern of USS *Lexington* is viewed as the carrier transits the Miraflores Locks on March 25, 1928. The three life-net booms on the stern would be removed from the ship sometime during the next year. Next to the center boom, a ventilator door is open.

After reporting to the Battle Fleet's headquarters at Long Beach, California, in early April 1928, *Lexington* proceeded to Hunters Point Naval Shipyard at San Francisco for repairs and maintenance. In this photograph the carrier is seen in drydock number 3 at Hunters Point on April 19. The building with the curved side adjacent to *Lexington* is building number 140, the pumphouse for drydock 3. *National Museum of Naval Aviation*

Lexington, center, is viewed in drydock 3 at Hunters Point in a photograph dated April 19, 1928. A close examination of the flight deck suggests that crewmen were applying new stain to it. To the left, another ship is in drydock number 2.

Lexington is viewed from the front in drydock 3 at Hunters Point. Between the drydocks, the structure with the smokestack is the pumphouse that extracted the water from drydock 2 when a ship was brought into that dock. Both drydocks still exist.

A photo dated April 21, 1928, shows *Lexington* in drydock at Hunters Point from the aft port quarter. Two vertical shores or braces support the weight of the stern. Staging planks for the workmen are suspended from rigging attached to fittings built into the hull. Farther up on the side of the hull are two boat booms in their stowed positions. The brackets on the hull to which the heels, or bottoms, of those booms are hinged are visible.

Aircraft are parked on *Lexington's* flight deck during April 1928. Two Curtiss Hawks with weatherproof covers over their cowls are to the right. Farther back are Martin T3M torpedo bombers. All planes are secured to the flight deck with rope stays. *Naval History and Heritage Command*

A variety of plane types are on the flight deck in this ca. 1928 photo. In the foreground are Vought O2U Corsairs of VS-3B. Aft of them are three Loening Amphibians of Utility Squadron 1 (VJ-1), with landing gear that retracted into the central float structure. *San Diego Air and Space Museum*

Lexington makes a full-power run off the Southern California coast on May 24, 1928. Such test runs were conducted when the ship was new, and at later intervals to check the ability of the engines and boilers to maintain full speed for over a period of time.

An aerial view of *Lexington* during a full-power run in late May 1928 shows the significant wake the ship churned up. The light-colored cross on the forward part of the flight deck was a temporary feature, possibly intended as a calibration marking.

With the palisade erected in the foreground to cut down on wind, crewmen of *Lexington* scrub their hammocks in the time-honored naval fashion in 1928 of using long-handled brushes and soapy water. They will then hang them to dry on the rails. *National Museum of Naval Aviation*

A bow-on shot of *Lexington* portrays her power as she cuts through the waves during speed trials off Southern California on June 18, 1928. The ship set a new record speed of 30 knots during the trials, but her sister ship, *Saratoga*, broke the record the next month. *National Museum of Naval Aviation*

A photographer in a passing Navy plane took this shot of the port amidships area of *Lexington* in June 1928. Both of the elevators are lowered, but the flap doors immediately aft of the forward elevator are raised flush with the flight deck. When lowered, those flaps swung down at right angles into the open space in the main-deck level below. To the left, gun crewmen are gathered around the forward port 5-inch/25-caliber mounts; the aft mount is trained inboard.

Some of *Lexington's* defensive artillery is viewed. In the foreground are the three starboard forward 5-inch/25-caliber mounts. The semicircular platform extensions were hinged so they could be stored folded up. To the rear are the forward 8-inch gun mounts. *San Diego Air and Space Museum*

Six months after her first drydocking at Hunters Point, *Lexington* returned on October 31, 1928, for more work. The semicircular platform extensions seen lowered in the preceding photo of the starboard forward gallery are seen raised on the port forward gallery.

It is George Washington's birthday, February 22, 1929, and USS *Lexington* is in full dress, decked out in flags and pennants fore to aft, off Panama. Dressing a ship is the Navy's way of honoring holidays and special events. Boat booms are extended from the hull.

Ship signal flags

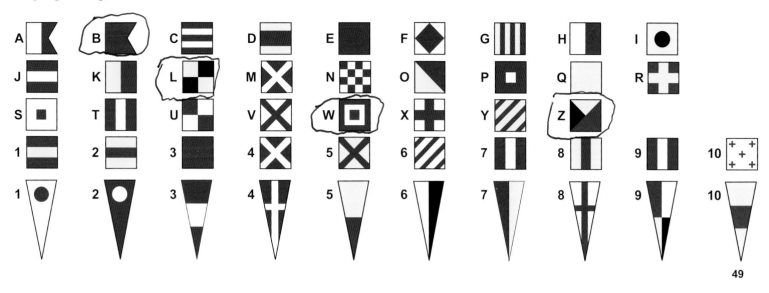

49

Toward the top of *Lexington's* foremast is the forward secondary-battery control top, from which the 5-inch gun batteries were remotely controlled. At the bottom of the photo is the forward primary-battery control top, from which the 8-inch guns were directed.

On March 7, 1929, crewmen swab *Lexington's* deck. One man sprays water on the wooden deck while others scrub it with long-handled brushes. With well over 100,000 square feet of area on the flight deck, swabbing this deck was a serious, time-consuming business. *National Archives via Rob Stern*

The twin 8-inch guns of turret number 1 are viewed from below, with one of the guns of turret number 2 visible between them. The 8-inch/55-caliber designation of these guns meant that the guns had a bore of 8 inches and a length of fifty-five times their bore, or 440 inches. Fitted in the muzzles of the guns are tompions, large plugs that kept out salt, moisture, and foreign objects. Visible in the background, top to bottom, are the radio-compass booth, forward main-battery control top, and forward secondary-battery control top.

A Vought O2U-2 Corsair takes off from *Lexington* in March 1929. Although the carrier originally had a catapult for launching seaplanes, for other planes the procedure was to steer the ship into the wind, thus increasing the airflow and enabling short takeoffs.

USS *Lexington's* number 3 twin 8-inch gun mount, immediately aft of the smokestack, is being fired during exercises. The twin 8-inch/55-caliber Mk. 9 Mod. 1 guns normally were remotely controlled by the fore and aft fire-control directors.

A photo dated October 7, 1929, shows the effects of the 8-inch guns of turret number 2 on a target screen. The crews of the 8-inch guns of the main battery as well as of the ship's other guns built and maintained proficiency by frequent target practice.

In October 1929, *Lexington* made the first of many visits to the Navy Yard, Puget Sound (NYPS), at Bremerton, Washington, for refitting, maintenance, and repairs. The carrier is shown moored to a dock at NYPS in a photo dated October 14.

Martin T4M-1 BuNo A-7638 was assigned to the leader of the third section of VT-1 in 1929. The T4M-1 had a maximum speed of 114 miles per hour, a range of 363 miles, and armament of a torpedo and one flex-mounted .30-caliber machine gun in the rear cockpit.

Curtiss F6C-3 Hawk BuNo A-7149 of VB-1B "Red Rippers" served on *Lexington*. The F6C-4 had a maximum speed of 153 miles per hour, a range of 341 miles, and armament of two .30-caliber machine guns or one .30-caliber and one .50-caliber.

Lexington wears full dress on October 27, 1929, to celebrate Navy Day at NYPS, Bremerton. Coincidentally, the stock market crash that precipitated the Great Depression occurred just three days earlier, but NYPS would actually grow during the Depression.

Several Boeing fighter planes are undergoing major overhauls on the aft end of the hangar deck around 1929. Two fuselages are supported on wooden stands as mechanics work on them. In the background are several wings, including one upright at the center. *National Museum of Naval Aviation*

In a view of part of the flight deck of *Lexington* taken around 1929, in the foreground is a mix of Boeing F3B-1 fighter planes of VF-3B and Curtiss F6C-3 fighters of VB-1B. The F3B-1s are the planes with the radial engines with covers over them, while the F6C-3s are the ones with inline engines, propeller spinners, and no covers. In the background are Martin T4M-1 torpedo bombers assigned to VT-1B. The F3B-1 in the foreground with the white fuselage band was the plane of the leader of the second section of VF-3B. *National Museum of Naval Aviation*

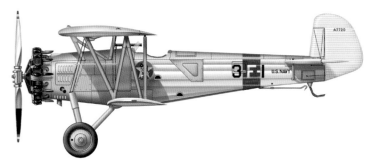

Boeing F3B-1 BuNo A-7720 served with VF-3B around 1929. The F3B-1 had a maximum speed of 157 miles per hour and a range of 340 miles. It was armed with two fixed .30-caliber machine guns and could carry up to 125 pounds of bombs.

Lexington rides at anchor in Commencement Bay, Tacoma, Washington, on December 16, 1929. She was there to generate electrical power for the city, which was suffering a shortage of hydroelectric power because an extended drought had lowered its reservoirs.

Once *Lexington* was moored at Baker Dock, Tacoma, connections were made from the carrier's bus bars to high-tension electrical lines the city had extended to that dock. *Lexington* supplied electricity to the city from December 17, 1929, to January 16, 1930. *National Museum of Naval Aviation*

An aerial view shows *Lexington* at Baker Dock on January 3, 1930, midway through her stay in Tacoma. By now, the abbreviation "LEX" had been painted on the aft end of her flight deck as an identification aid to returning pilots. A large circle was also present.

A barge holding a support made of timbers with insulators on top was placed between the port side of *Lexington* and Baker Dock to support the electrical cables routed through the door in the side of the hull (*right*) to transformers temporarily located on the dock. *National Archives Seattle via Tracey White*

The support and electrical cables seen in the preceding photo are visible on the barge toward the right of this photo dated December 18, 1929, taken from the flight deck of *Lexington*. To the center are transformer banks and circuit breakers on Baker Dock. *National Archives Seattle via Tracey White*

Lexington is moored to Baker Dock, Tacoma, on Christmas Eve 1929. During the monthlong visit of the carrier to Tacoma, the ship provided the city with 4.25 million kilowatt-hours of electrical power. Complex measures were needed during the operation to ensure safety. *National Archives Seattle via Tracey White*

Lexington continues to provide electrical power to the city of Tacoma on January 13, 1930, a few days before her departure. By now, winter rains had replenished the city's reservoirs, and the dams would begin to generate hydroelectric power once again.

In a February 21, 1930, view of *Lexington's* air group, front and center is Vought O2U side number 3-B-1, assigned to the squadron leader of VS-3B. To the bottom left are two of the ship's 6-pounder saluting guns; at the top left is the secondary conning station. *National Museum of Naval Aviation*

USS *Lexington* passes through the Pedro Miguel Locks of the Panama Canal on February 28, 1930, en route from the West Coast to the Caribbean, where she would participate with the Black Force in Fleet Problem X, war games that began on March 10.

A crowd of civilians watch as *Lexington*, *right*, negotiates the Gatun Locks of the Panama Canal. The 5-inch/25-caliber guns of the aft starboard gallery are at full elevation, and the semicircular platform extensions of the gallery are raised to provide clearance. *San Diego Air and Space Museum*

A rangefinder crew is at its station on one of the wings of a secondary-battery (or 5-inch gun) control top on *Lexington* in March 1930. A rangefinder was mounted on each wing of the platform, and in the middle of the platform were two 5-inch directors.

With aircraft wings and a radial aircraft engine framing the scene in the foreground, the upper part of the superstructure and the foremast are in view. At the bottom is the aft part of the flag plot; above it are a searchlight platform and the forward gun control tops. On the wings of the 5-inch gun control top, enclosed with canvas windbreaks, are the two forward 5-inch rangefinders, such as the one illustrated in the preceding photo.

USS *Lexington* rests at anchor at Hampton Roads, Virginia, in May 1930. A good view is provided of the configuration of the life nets that extended around the sides of the hull just below the flight deck. Crewmen are swabbing the forward part of the flight deck.

USS *Lexington* is tied up alongside Pier 15, Balboa, Canal Zone, on June 29, 1930, on her voyage west to rejoin the Pacific Fleet. The pre–World War II exercises and fleet problems necessitated many transits of the Panama Canal.

Lexington negotiates the Gatun Locks of the Panama Canal on March 24,1931, once again bound for fleet exercises in the Caribbean. Suspended from the boom next to the smokestack is a booth for the ship's pilot, the better to con the ship thorough the locks.

During a break from maneuvers in the Caribbean on March 31, 1931, USS *Lexington* rests at anchor at the US Navy base at Guantánamo Bay, Cuba. Within the next few days, *Lexington* would commence the return trip via the Panama Canal to California.

USS *Lexington* approaches a dock at Balboa, the Panama Canal Zone, on April 7, 1931, during her return trip from the Caribbean to California. Visible ahead of the bow of *Lexington* in the distance is the forward part of USS *Saratoga*, moored at Pier 16.

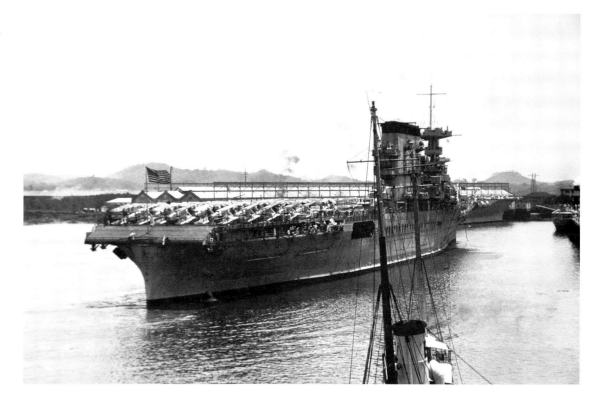

Lexington and other ships of the Battle Fleet are anchored at Lahaina Roads off the west coast of Maui in mid-February 1932. The Battle Fleet recently had sailed from California to the Hawaiian Islands to participate in a fleet exercise, a simulated attack on the islands. *National Museum of Naval Aviation*

Sailors and officers of USS *Lexington* are assembled for review on the afterpart of the flight deck in March 1932. In the left foreground are F3B-1s of VF-2B, while in the background are Martin T4M-1s of VT-1B. To the right is a plane of VF-5B. *Naval History and Heritage Command*

A March 1932 photo of the forward part of *Lexington's* flight deck shows four Boeing F3B-1s of VF-2B in the foreground. In the background are Vought SU-2 Corsairs assigned to Marine Scouting Squadron 15 and aircraft with markings for VS-3B. *National Museum of Naval Aviation*

In a view overlooking *Lexington's* aft 8-inch guns, Martin T4M-1s of VT-1B warm their engines preparatory to takeoff. The date was March 14, 1932, during Fleet Problem XIII. The large circle painted on the flight deck during this period is visible.

On May 11, 1932, fifteen welding machines were operated in parallel to heat the stator winding of "D" generator. The stator was the stationary part of the turbogenerator's rotor system. This arrangement of welding rigs supplied 4,000 amps at 12 volts.

Lexington is in drydock in December 1932, and workmen are preparing the lower part of the hull for painting. The staging the men are standing on is supported by rigging attached to permanent fittings in the hull; one such fitting is above the man to the far left. *National Archives via Rob Stern*

In early 1933, *Lexington* was in the Territory of Hawaii for Fleet Problem XIV. She is seen here off Honolulu, with Diamond Head in the distance. To the left in the second row of planes is what appears to be the Grumman XFF-1 prototype, then assigned to VF-5B.

Workmen at the Navy Yard, Puget Sound, in Bremerton, Washington, are pulling the starboard outboard propeller during a refitting and repair session in drydock in December 1932. The cone of the propeller has been removed and is lying below the scaffolding. A chain fall is rigged above the propeller to hoist it free of its mounting. Whenever the ship was in drydock, the propellers were carefully inspected for damage or wear.

In March 1933, *Lexington* is anchored off Long Beach, California, her air group neatly parked on the deck. Sometime before this photo was taken, her sister ship, *Saratoga*, got a vertical black stripe on each side of the smokestack to distinguish her from *Lexington*.

A Vought SU-2 Corsair scout plane assigned to Marine Scouting Squadron 15 (VS-15M) takes off from *Lexington* in March 1933. At that time, VS-15M was deployed with *Lexington*. The USMC insignia is on the side of the fuselage, below the aft cockpit.

Martin BM-1 torpedo bomber BuNo A-8881 served with VT-1S on *Lexington* in 1932. The BM-1 had a top speed of 146 miles per hour and a range of 413 miles and carried one fixed and one flex-mounted .30-caliber machine gun and a torpedo or a 1,000-pound bomb.

One of *Lexington's* photographers took this moody view of the carrier docked at Bremerton, Washington, on October 20, 1933. In the 1930s, *Lexington* and her sister ship, *Saratoga*, frequently would come to Bremerton late in the year for refitting and repairs.

In a December 1933 photo of the port side of *Lexington's* superstructure, on the navigating bridge above the ladder next to the conning tower (*at lower left*) are red, yellow, and green lights the flight deck control officer used to signal planes preparing to take off.

In spring 1934, *Lexington* was deployed to the East Coast. During that voyage, the ship is seen navigating the Gatun Locks of the Panama Canal on April 23. The black paint of the band around the top of the smokestack also carried over to the top of the stack.

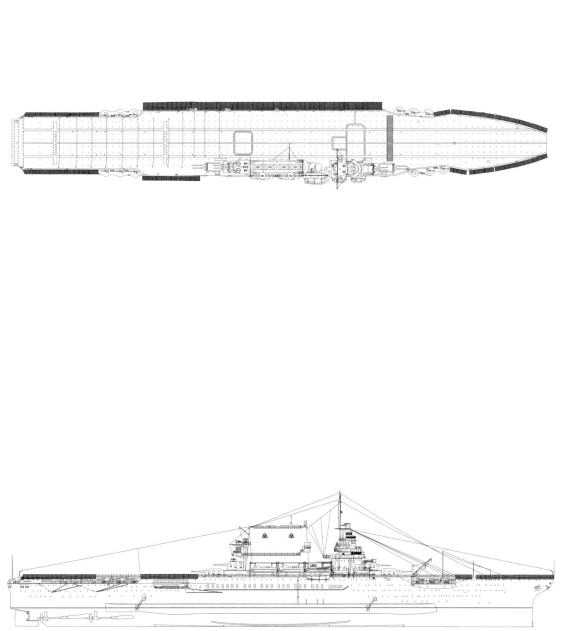

To the casual observer, *Lexington* in 1934 was little changed from her appearance during her commissioning seven years earlier. The forward flight deck still followed the lines of her finely tapered battle cruiser bow, and—strangely for a floating airfield—few antiaircraft weapons were present. Perhaps the most visible variance from her 1927 commissioning configuration was the broad black band painted around the top of the ship's funnel, which housed the four huge uptakes that exhausted her sixteen Yarrow boilers. *Lexington's* sister ship, *Saratoga*, received a broad vertical band on her funnel at the same time. These distinguishing markings were added to aid aviators in finding their "home"—with the two nearly identical ships often operating together, aviator confusion about the vessels' identity had been an ongoing problem.

However, while little had changed externally on the ship itself, *Lexington's* main armament—her aircraft—had changed considerably during her seven years of service. For example, the F3B-1, T4M-1, F6C-2/3, and O2U-2 that she had borne during the 1929 Fleet Problem IX had given way to a succession of newer aircraft, such that by the time Fleet Problem XV was held in 1934, an all-new air group was being carried. For this fleet problem, *Lexington's* VT-1B was piloting the Martin BM-1/2, VS-3B and VS-14M were both flying the Vought SU-2/3 aircraft, VF-5B was equipped with Grumman FF-1 fighters, and VF-2B was taking to the air in Boeing F4B-2 fighters.

Lexington's turboelectric propulsion gave the carrier the ability to move in reverse at speed, which also gave her the ability to launch aircraft from the rear of the flight deck, as demonstrated by a Martin BM torpedo bomber of VT-1B on May 17, 1934.

Officers and crewmen of Lexington man the rail, a naval tradition to render honors, as the ship passes in review for President Franklin Roosevelt off New York Harbor on May 31, 1934. Lexington was part of the largest USN peacetime armada to date.

A mass of airplanes parked on the flight deck of USS Lexington on May 26, 1934, includes in the foreground new Grumman FF-1 fighters of VF-5B. To the lower left is the aircraft of the leader of section 2 of that squadron, signified by the white fuselage band.

Lexington is approaching the Portsmouth Navy Yard on July 13, 1934, during her deployment that summer to the East Coast. Worthy of notice is that although the forward elevator is raised, the flap doors just aft of it are lowered.

Sister ships USS *Lexington*, *left*, and USS *Saratoga* are moored at Pier 90 in Manhattan in early July 1934, hosting throngs of visitors who came down to tour the ships. Planes of their air groups were aboard, increasing the interest of a tour of the Navy's big carriers. *National Museum of Naval Aviation*

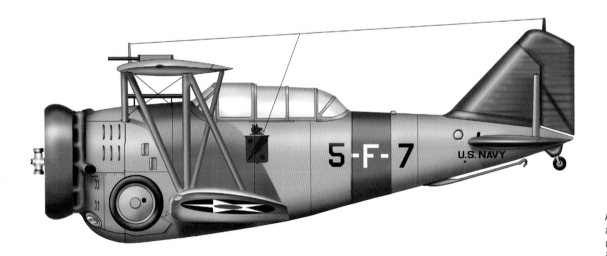

A Grumman SF-1 scout plane appears in the colors and markings of VF-5B "Red Rippers" in 1934. The SF-1 had a maximum speed of 206 miles per hour, a range of 732 miles, and armament of one fixed and one flex-mounted .30-caliber machine gun.

Aircraft are crowded into the hangar deck of USS *Lexington* around 1935. To the left are several aircraft fuselages suspended from the ceiling of the hangar. The practice of stowing aircraft overhead in the hangar as a space-saving measure was called tricing. *San Diego Air and Space Museum*

Lexington is observed from her port side on June 5, 1935, toward the end of Fleet Problem XVI, which saw the carrier operating in Hawaiian waters with the fleet. Within a few months, *Lexington* would undergo a refit that would give her smokestack a different look.

Arrestor hook extended, a Grumman SF-1 scout plane piloted by a Cmdr. Webb comes in for a landing on USS *Lexington* on May 12, 1935. Although the side number of the aircraft is difficult to discern, it is likely this plane was assigned to VS-3B.

A Grumman F2F-1 fighter takes off from *Lexington* on May 31, 1935. This aircraft probably was assigned to VF-2B, which is known to have been flying the F2F-1 from *Lexington* at that time. In the background is a Grumman JF-1 Duck amphibian plane.

In the late summer of 1935, *Lexington* underwent a refitting at the Navy Yard, Puget Sound, Bremerton, Washington, the main focus of which was the ship's antiaircraft defenses, with five machine gun platforms being added to the ship. Four platforms were built onto the sides of the hull below the level of the flight deck, two near the stern and two near the bow. Each of these was intended to hold four .50-caliber machine gun mounts. A fifth platform encircled the upper part of the smokestack and was designed to hold six .50-caliber machine guns per side. The smokestack platform and the forward starboard platform are visible in this photo taken on September 25, 1935, at Bremerton. *National Archives via Rob Stern*

In a bow-on view on September 25, 1935, the new forward machine gun platforms jut from the sides of the hull, with temporary staging rigged below them. The radio-compass booth has been removed from below the 8-inch gun control compartment. *National Archives via Rob Stern*

The new aft port machine gun platform on *Lexington*, just forward of the ship's nameplate, is viewed facing forward. Below the platform is temporary staging. The new machine gun platform around the upper part of the funnel is visible in the distance. *National Archives via Rob Stern*

Another photo taken on September 24, 1935, to document the new construction on *Lexington* shows the forward port machine gun platform. The twenty-eight .50-caliber machine gun mounts added during this refitting would provide a close-range defense against aircraft. *National Archives via Rob Stern*

Lexington lies at anchor off the coast of Panama on May 11, 1936, during Fleet Problem XVII. During these annual fleet exercises, the crew of *Lexington* would gain crucial experience that would serve them and the rest of the Navy well when war came. *Lexington* was still carrying several seaplanes, and two of them are parked to the front of the forward elevator. Both that elevator and the flap doors aft of it are lowered, exposing the T shape of the elevator well.

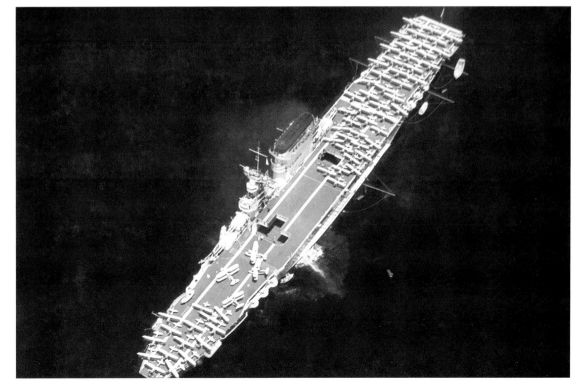

Off Long Beach, California, on September 17, 1936, a Goodyear blimp hovers over USS *Lexington* as the ship's crew, dressed in whites, spells out "NAVY" on the flight deck. The machine gun platform on the smokestack casts a shadow on the side of the stack. *National Museum of Naval Aviation*

On November 12, 1936, *Lexington* steams through San Francisco Bay, with Alcatraz Island in the background. The ship was visiting the area to participate in the opening of the San Francisco–Oakland Bay Bridge, which was opened to traffic on that date.

Throughout her career, *Lexington* most often steamed from California ports. For overhaul and heavy maintenance, she typically ventured north to Washington's Navy Yard Puget Sound. In 1936, *Lexington* tied up to the dock at the massive complex, where she underwent significant modifications and flight deck changes. *National Archives Seattle via Tracy White*

The most significant change in *Lexington's* appearance prior to World War II, and some would argue the most significant change altogether, was the result of a late 1936–early 1937 refit at Puget Sound. One of the most significant modifications made during that refit involved the widening of the flight deck forward and the installation of additional arrestor gear. These changes allowed flight operations to be conducted from either end of the ship. Previously, the narrow forward flight deck was fine for launching aircraft, but recovering aircraft over the bow was challenging, even more so with the lack of arresting wires oriented for this purpose.

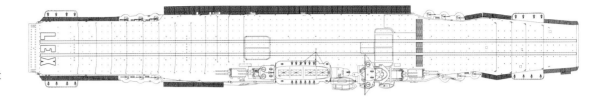

During a refitting at the Navy Yard, Puget Sound, in early 1937, *Lexington* had the front end of her flight deck widened. This modification made landings feasible on the front of the flight deck, and arrestor gear was installed there as well. On the forward end of the flight deck, several Grumman airplanes are visible, probably F2F-1s. Aft of the gun gallery, above the waterline, is a door in the hull with an access ladder where boats could embark and disembark passengers. *US Naval Shipbuilding Museum*

In this photo of *Lexington* from off her bow, the center anchor has been lowered. The three forward anchors were raised and lowered by a windlass located on the main deck just below the forward part of the flight deck. Chain lockers were below the windlass. *National Museum of Naval Aviation*

A March 1937 photo shows a landing signal officer's platform and windscreen along the forward part of the flight deck. This station was designed to be used should the aft part of the flight deck be damaged, and aircraft were recovered on the front of the deck.

Crash barriers were the last resort for stopping a landing aircraft should the aircraft fail to catch an arrestor wire with its hook. To the left of center in this photo is the port number 3 crash barrier stanchion, from which the barrier wires were rigged. Behind the stanchion is some of the combination life net / windbreaker mounted alongside parts of the flight deck. The crisscrossing canvas material cut down on the winds that blew across the deck.

Alongside the flight deck of *Lexington* there were several control stations for operating the arresting wires. Shown here in a photograph dated March 26, 1937, is control station 6, located on the starboard side of the flight deck forward of the aircraft crane (*top left*). It consisted of a small platform with safety chains and stanchions, and controls and gauges for operating the arresting gear. To the far left is the muzzle of one of the 5-inch/25-caliber guns.

Control station number 4, where arrestor wires 5 and 7 were operated, is viewed on March 28, 1937, with the safety chains and stanchions removed. Mounted on the edge of the flight deck are, left to right, an air-pressure gauge for the yielding elements of the arrestor gear, pneumatic controls for the yielding elements of wires 5 and 7, pressure-control levers for the two wires, and the yielding element control levers for the wires.

At control station number 2, shown here, arrestor wires 2 and 4 were controlled. The controls and gauge are similar to those depicted in the preceding photograph, with a different location for the gauge and the pneumatic control levers.

Great Lakes BG-1 BuNo 9505 of VB-3B takes off from USS *Lexington* on May 23, 1937. This dive-bomber, of which only sixty were built, was powered by a Pratt & Whitney R-1535-82 radial engine and could carry a 1,000-pound bomb under the fuselage.

Landing signal officer Lt. R. S. Clark and his talker are on the LSO's platform behind the windscreen along the flight deck. Using his paddles, the LSO signaled approaching pilots if they were flying too high, too low, too fast, or too slow for a safe, uneventful landing.

On May 20, 1937, a Great Lakes BG-1 has just taken off from *Lexington* during fleet maneuvers off Hawaii. The BG-1 would have a short tenure on *Lexington* and would be replaced by the following year with the Vought SB2U-1 Vindicator dive-bomber.

Several Boeing F4B-4s are parked "tailed" up to the smokestack on USS *Lexington* on May 8, 1937. At the center of the photo, the diagonal port leg of the foremast is visible. To the far left, parts of the gunhouses of the twin 8-inch gun turrets are in view.

A Martin M-130 flying boat passes over the bow of USS *Lexington* off Hawaii on May 19, 1937. Grumman F2F-1s of VF-2B "Flying Chiefs" are lined up on the forward end of the flight deck. This squadron had been the first to transition to the Grumman F2F-1.

Vought SBU-1 Corsair BuNo 9760 served with VS-3B on *Lexington* in 1937. The SBU-1 had a maximum speed of 205 miles per hour, a range of 477 miles, and armament of two fixed and one flex-mounted .30-caliber machine guns and 500 pounds of bombs.

Lexington was participating in small-scale war games in company with USS *Saratoga* and USS *Ranger* (CV-4) when photographed on February 16, 1938. The carrier was wearing a large letter E on the smokestack in honor of winning the annual fleet-wide competition for engineering excellence. From this angle, the absence of the radio-compass booth below the 8-inch control compartment, which was removed in 1935, is apparent.

USS *Lexington* was photographed from USS *Ranger* in March 1938. That month these ships participated in the annual war games, Fleet Problem XIX. The purpose of that year's fleet problem was to test the defenses both of Hawaii and San Francisco. By this time, the US Navy considered a war with Japan to be a very likely possibility, and the annual fleet problems were designed to test the Navy's offensive and defensive theories and prepare the fleet for the most likely scenarios should war come.

In March 1938, during Fleet Problem XIX USS *Lexington* is anchored off Honolulu, with Diamond Head visible in the distance. During this exercise, the air groups from *Lexington* and *Saratoga* successfully "attacked" Pearl Harbor and, later, San Francisco.

Lexington displays the E award for engineering excellence on her smokestack around 1938. Visible at the base of the smokestack and to its immediate front are three barges; three other boats are on davits amidships, and one appears to be in the boat pocket. *US Naval Shipbuilding Museum*

Around 1939, *Lexington* is conducting aircraft recovery operations. An airplane is coming in for a landing, and planes that have landed are being grouped to the front of the flight deck. Carrier-based aircraft at this date were still preponderantly biplanes. *National Museum of Naval Aviation*

Lexington is viewed from above in another photo taken around 1939. The light-colored aircraft contrast strongly with the carrier's flight deck. Once the United States went to war, efforts would be made to match the colors of the flight deck and the aircraft. *National Museum of Naval Aviation*

In February 1939, *Lexington* returned to the Caribbean for Fleet Problem XX, a simulation of the defense of the East Coast of the United States. President Roosevelt observed the maneuvers. Here, *Lexington* is at anchor at Guantánamo Bay, Cuba. *National Museum of Naval Aviation*

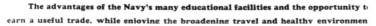

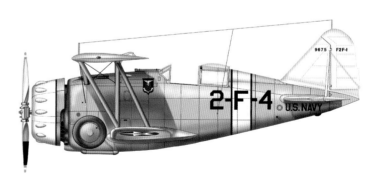

A US Navy poster released in November 1939 included scenes of life in the Navy and, to the lower left of the sailor at the center, a view of USS *Lexington*. The poster appealed to recruits' desire to gain a free education, travel to exotic locales, and learn a trade. *Naval History and Heritage Command*

Grumman F2F-1 BuNo 9675 appears in markings for VF-2 "Flying Chiefs" serving on USS *Lexington* in early 1940. The F2F-1 had a maximum speed of 231 miles per hour, a range of 750 miles, and armament of two .30-caliber machine guns.

The Navy Yard, Puget Sound, at Bremerton, Washington, was a busy yard in the 1930s and would become much busier once the United States entered World War II. It was a key base for the refitting and repair of Navy ships. Even when this photo was taken in 1940, it was a beehive of activity, with numerous ships moored to docks and sitting in drydocks. One of those ships is USS *Lexington*, toward the bottom of the photograph. *National Archives San Bruno via Tracey White*

Following a visit to San Francisco Bay in 1940, USS *Lexington* passes under the Golden Gate Bridge on its way to the ocean. Her air group would land on her after the carrier cleared the Golden Gate. "LEX" is still painted on the aft end of the flight deck. *National Archives San Bruno via Tracey White*

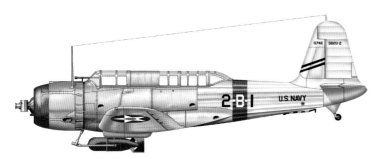

Vought SB2U-2 BuNo 0746 was the aircraft of the commander of VB-2 on *Lexington* in 1939. The SB2U-2 had a maximum speed of 252 miles per hour, a range of 1,002 miles, and armament of one fixed and one flex-mounted .50-caliber machine gun and 1,000 pounds of bombs.

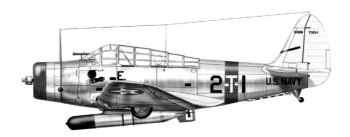

The commander of VT-2 flew this Douglas TBD-1 Devastator in 1938. It had a maximum speed of 206 miles per hour and had a range of 700 miles, and carried one fixed .30- or .50-caliber machine gun, one flex .30-caliber, and a Mk. XIII torpedo or 1,200 pounds of bombs.

Brewster F2A-2 BuNo 1415 served with VF-2 on *Lexington* in spring 1941. It had a maximum speed of 344 miles per hour and a range of 1,670 miles and mounted four fixed .50-caliber machine guns and provisions for two 100-pound bombs.

A Brewster F2A-3 of VF-2 appears in a camouflage scheme from January 1942 of Nonspecular Blue Gray over Light Gray. The F2A-3 had similar armament to the F2A-2. It had a maximum speed of 323 miles per hour and a maximum range of 965 miles.

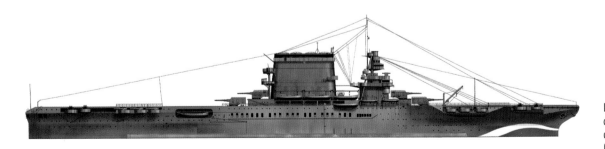

In October 1941, *Lexington* had a camouflage scheme of a combination of Measure 1—Dark Gray on vertical surfaces up to the top of the funnel, and 5-L Light Gray above that level—and Measure 5, which entailed a white false wave painted on each side of the bow.

Lexington steams off San Diego in October 1941. She is painted in the combination of Measures 1 and 5, with the false bow wave prominent. The purpose of this false wave was to give the enemy a false idea of the ship's actual speed, which usually was necessary in their targeting calculations. Later in October the ship was repainted in Measure 12, a graded scheme with Sea Blue up to the level of the hangar deck and Ocean Gray from there to the top of the superstructure.

CHAPTER 2
World War II and Loss

Although the Japanese attack on Pearl Harbor on December 7, 1941, was a highly successful operation, one of their primary objectives went completely unfulfilled. The Japanese planners had sought to decimate the entire US carrier force, but none of the American carriers were present that day.

Lexington had sailed from Pearl Harbor on December 5, carrying Marine Scout Bomber Squadron 231 to Midway, to bolster the island's defenses. *Lexington* was 425 miles from her destination when word of the Japanese surprise attack reached her small task force. *Lexington* immediately began to search for the Japanese fleet, but no contact was made, so *Lexington* and Task Force 12 rendezvoused with *Enterprise*'s Task Force 8, continuing the search until all the ships returned to Pearl Harbor on December 13.

The next day, *Lexington* sailed again, first toward Jaluit in the Marshall Islands, and then redirected toward Wake Island. However, Wake fell to the Japanese before *Lexington*, *Saratoga*, and *Enterprise* could reach the island. *Lexington* turned around and returned to Pearl Harbor on December 27.

A relatively quiet period followed as *Lexington* and her crew conducted routine operations until February 20, 1942. During that time, *Lexington* attacked a suspected Japanese submarine on January 10, and *Lexington*'s supporting fleet oiler, *Neches*, was sunk by the Japanese submarine *I-72* on January 23.

On February 20, 1942, as *Lexington* was sailing to attack Japanese forces based on Rabaul, she was attacked by two waves of Mitsubishi G4M "Betty" bombers of the Japanese 4th Air Group. Normally the G4Ms would have attacked with torpedoes, but none were available, so the Bettys each carried a pair of 550-pound bombs. Of the nine bombers in the first wave, only four reached the carrier to make their attacks. None of their bombs hit *Lexington*,

and the entire first wave was shot ultimately shot down. Only five of the eight Bettys of the second wave reached *Lexington*, and again they scored no hits. Only three of the seventeen G4Ms returned to their base.

Lexington's Combat Air Patrol truly saved the day, downing fourteen of the seventeen attacking Japanese planes. On that day, Lt. Edward "Butch" O'Hare, flying an F4F Wildcat, was credited with downing five of the Japanese bombers attacking *Lexington*. Not only did the feat earn O'Hare the title of "ace," in a single day, but he also became the first naval aviator to win the Medal of Honor.

After fifty-four days in the combat zone (including a March 10 attack on New Guinea), *Lexington* returned to Pearl Harbor on March 26. *Lexington* underwent repairs, and major modifications were made to her armament. One of the most visible changes made to the ship was the removal of her four two-gun, 8-inch/55-caliber turrets. These were to be replaced by four dual-purpose, 5-inch, 38-caliber twin mounts, which would substantially bolster the carrier's antiaircraft defenses. The Japanese attack on Pearl Harbor had demonstrated that the carrier was unlikely to be involved in a surface action, and a powerful, long-range antiaircraft battery had become a necessity.

Unfortunately, the 5-inch, 38-caliber mounts for *Lexington* were not available at Pearl Harbor until early April 1942, so she put to sea on April 15 with seven 1.1-inch AA guns in quad mounts instead. *Lexington*'s old 8-inch turrets were not discarded; rather, they were given to the Army, which installed them as coastal defense batteries Wilridge and Opaeula in Hawaii, where they remained until scrapped in 1948.

After leaving the shipyard in April 1942, *Lexington* transported VMF-211 (and their F2A Buffalo fighters) to Palmyra Atoll and conducted training operations for the ship's crew. By the end of the month, operations were in motion that would send *Lexington* to the Coral Sea, and her fate.

Acting on orders from Adm. Nimitz, *Lexington*, *Yorktown*, and several escorting vessels were sent to the Coral Sea to defend Tulagi and Port Moresby. On May 7, 1942, *Lexington* would take part in the US Navy's first carrier-versus-carrier combat action. At 0815 hours, the main Japanese force was believed to be located just 175 miles north of *Lexington*'s position. Seventy-one minutes later, *Lexington* launched her attack aircraft, and Yorktown followed suit about thirty minutes later. At about 1100 hours, *Lexington*'s strike force attacked the Japanese carrier *Shōhō*, with *Yorktown*'s bombers joining in shortly afterward. In all, ninety-three US Navy aircraft savaged the Japanese ship. An estimated seven torpedoes and thirteen 1,000-pound bombs found their mark, sending *Shōhō* beneath the waves just thirty-six minutes after the first strike.

But little *Shōhō* was not alone, and at 1630 the large carriers *Shōkaku* and *Zuikaku* launched their aircraft to avenge her loss. However, the Japanese strike force of twelve dive-bombers and fifteen torpedo bombers failed to find the American carriers and were themselves attacked by the US Combat Air Patrol. Nine Japanese bombers were downed for the cost of two American fighters. As the sun sank low in the sky, some of the surviving Japanese spotted the American carriers but, rather than attacking, mistook them for their own and attempted to land, an effort that ended in their destruction.

At dawn on May 8, *Lexington*'s aircraft began hunting for the Japanese carriers, hoping to replicate the previous day's success. The Japanese carriers were soon located, and at 0915 both *Lexington* and *Yorktown* attacked. Unfortunately, the results were not as good as the day before, and just *Shōkaku* received moderate damage. Worse, the returning US aircraft were trailed by the Japanese, who pinpointed the location both of *Lexington* and *Yorktown* and launched their own strike force of ninety planes.

In the ensuing attack, eight torpedoes were launched at *Yorktown*, but through superb seamanship she avoided all of them. The considerably greater size of *Lexington*, however, made her less responsive and thus an easier target. She was struck by two of the eleven torpedoes the Japanese launched at her. Then two Japanese dive-bombers scored hits on *Lexington*, striking the port forward 5-inch ammunition locker as well as the ship's funnel. Despite the damages, the carrier's great strength and her valiant damage control parties kept *Lexington* in fighting form for an hour and fifteen minutes after her last attacker retired. Unfortunately, gasoline vapors collected, and when they ignited, the resulting explosions and fires doomed the ship.

At 1707. Capt. Sherman ordered the crew to abandon ship. He remained on board until all his crew were off the ship. The American task force was able to rescue nearly 2,770 men from *Lexington*. At approximately 1915 the destroyer *Phelps* closed in and fired five torpedoes to sink the great ship.

Lexington remained lost until March 5, 2018, when the crew of the research vessel *Petrel*, owned by Microsoft cofounder and philanthropist Paul G. Allen, found the remains of the carrier 1,000 meters below the surface of the Coral Sea. Her resting place is about 500 miles off the eastern coast of Australia. She is broken into four main sections, scattered over a mile on the seafloor.

APPROX. 3·400

An aerial view of Ford Island was taken by the US Navy during a November 1941 photographic survey of Pearl Harbor. Moored to the lower right is USS *Lexington*; although this side of Ford Island was where the aircraft carriers moored when in the harbor, *Lexington* was the only carrier present on that date. On Ford Island was Naval Air Station Ford Island. On December 7, 1941, *Lexington* was at sea and thus escaped the fate of the ships on Battleship Row to the upper left.

At the end of March 1942, *Lexington's* four 8-inch gun turrets were removed from the ship to make way for a battery of 1.1-inch automatic antiaircraft guns. In this photograph of that operation, turret number 1 is hovering over the already removed turret 2, suspended from the massive hammerhead crane at Pearl Harbor. The dock holding the crane was specially reinforced for the occasion, and similarly reinforced barges were used to transport the turrets once removed. *Naval History and Heritage Command*

Turret number 3 is being hoisted from its mounting on March 30, 1942. Of interest at the bottom of the photo are details of the ventilator doors. These were of French-door construction, whereby the entire door or just the upper half could be opened as required. *Naval History and Heritage Command*

Turret 3 is suspended in air and will soon be deposited on a barge lying next to *Lexington*. Projecting from the upper rear of the gunhouse of the turret is the left hood of the rangefinder, which was used when the gun mount was under local control. *Naval History and Heritage Command*

With hoist lines slung under the gun barrels and attached to the gunhouse, turret 3 has been landed on a barge next to *Lexington*. A Japanese invasion of Oahu was still considered a possibility, and the US Army needed them for its coastal defenses. *Naval History and Heritage Command*

Turret number 1 has been landed on special timber cribbing on the dock next to *Lexington* on March 31, 1942. The entire operation of removing the turrets from the ship took only four days. Marked on the front of the gunhouse is "Turret #1." *Naval History and Heritage Command*

On March 30, 1942, rigging is in place for hoisting turret number 3 clear of its mounting aft of the smokestack. Care was taken to avoid hitting the 8-inch fire-control station above the gunhouse of the turret. Antisplinter matting has been installed on the sides of the 8-inch fire-control station as well as on the 5-inch fire-control station above it. Toward the rear of the machine gun platform near the top of the smokestack is a 36-inch searchlight. *Naval History and Heritage Command*

With *Lexington* looming in the background, turrets 1 and 2 sit on a dock, and in front of them, two barbette foundation stools rest on a barge in the foreground. The gunhouse of one of the turrets is hidden behind the barbette foundation stool to the right. *Naval History and Heritage Command*

Lexington from the stern to the forward end of the superstructure is viewed during the ship's refitting at Pearl Harbor on March 31, 1942. During this refit, the ship received other modifications, including the addition of twenty-two 20 mm antiaircraft gun mounts, most of which were installed on four new antiaircraft-gun galleries: one on the starboard side of the base of the smokestack, two in the boat pocket on the port side of the hull, and one in the starboard boat pocket. *Naval History and Heritage Command*

Lexington's 8-inch turrets enjoyed a second life as US Army coastal-defense guns on the island of Oahu. Her sister ship, *Saratoga*, also transferred its 8-inch turrets to the Army in early 1942. One of the turrets formerly of those carriers is seen to the right. *US Army Museum of Hawaii*

An army corporal stands next to one of the 8-inch turrets from the Lexington-class carriers recycled as a coastal-defense gun mount. Those turrets were emplaced at four installations on Oahu: Batteries Burgess, Kirkpatrick, Ricker, and Riggs. *US Army Museum of Hawaii*

Visible through the shipyard machinery and equipment in the foreground is USS *Lexington* on April 13, 1942, during her refitting at Pearl Harbor. Several noteworthy details are visible on the ship. Antisplinter matting is present on the navigation bridge and possibly on higher levels of the superstructure and battery-control stations as well. On the top front of the smokestack are a CXAM-1 "mattress" radar antenna installed in 1941, and a smoke deflector. The flag plot has been extended and the rangefinder moved from the top of the pilothouse to the top of the flag plot. *National Archives via James Noblin*

Two legendary pilots, Jimmy Thach, foreground, and Edward H. "Butch" O'Hare, of VF-3, fly their Grumman Wildcats in April 1942. O'Hare was awarded the Medal of Honor for shooting down five Japanese planes attacking *Lexington* on February 20, 1942. *Naval History and Heritage Command*

Members of *Lexington*'s Fighting Squadron 3 pose for a group photograph on March 5, 1942. This squadron, commanded by Lt. Cmdr. John S. "Jimmy" Thach, joined the ship's air group on January 27, 1942, and racked up an impressive record in the coming months. *Naval History and Heritage Command*

This Grumman F4F-3 of VF-3 was Lt. Cmdr. Thach's plane in spring 1942. It had a maximum speed of 331 miles per hour, a range of 845 miles, and armament of four wing-mounted. 50-caliber machine guns and could mount two 100-pound bombs.

This Douglas SBD-3 served with VS-2 in May 1942. The SBD-3 had a maximum speed of 250 miles per hour and a range of 1,560 miles and was armed with two fixed .50-caliber machine guns, one or two flex .30-caliber machine guns, and 1,600 pounds in bombs.

On April 15, 1942, *Lexington* left Pearl Harbor with Task Force 11, bound for the South Pacific. This force clashed with the Imperial Japanese Navy in the Battle of the Coral Sea. In this photo, *Lexington* is viewed from USS *Yorktown* (CV-5) during the battle. *Naval History and Heritage Command*

On May 7 at 1200, *Lexington's* air group, commanded by Cmdr. William B. Ault, struck a hard blow, hitting the IJN carrier *Shoho* with two 1,000-pound bombs and five torpedoes. After more attacks, Shoho sank. The next day *Lexington* would come under attack. *San Diego Air and Space Museum*

At about 1105 on the morning of May 8, 1942, in the Battle of the Coral Sea, Japanese aircraft located *Lexington* and soon commenced an attack on her. At 1120 they scored two torpedo hits on the port side of the carrier. In this photo, explosions wrack the ship. *Naval History and Heritage Command*

In this photograph, *Lexington* is under attack by Japanese dive-bombers on May 8 and is maneuvering in an attempt to dodge the bombs. Two bombs struck the ship, one killing the crew of a 5-inch antiaircraft gun and starting fires and another hitting the smokestack. *Naval History and Heritage Command*

Following the Japanese attack on *Lexington*, emergency crews put out the fires on deck, and the carrier was able to recover its air group, returning from attacks on the Japanese fleet, that afternoon. A crewman surveys damage to the forward port 5-inch gun gallery. *Naval History and Heritage Command*

Two crewmen survey the damage to 5-inch mount number 6 at the aft end of the forward port gallery. The damage to the gun gallery was caused by a bomb that pierced the deck just beyond these men and exploded in an ammunition locker one deck below. *Naval History and Heritage Command*

Damage to the forward port 5-inch guns is shown. Three men of the crew of 5-inch gun mount number 4, the one pointing outboard, were killed by the bomb blast. A second bomb that hit the ship struck on the port side of the smokestack, killing some crewmen. *National Archives via Rob Stern*

The forward port 5-inch gun gallery is viewed from its forward end, facing aft, in the aftermath of the attack. In the foreground is 5-inch mount number 2, with mount 4 just aft of it. *Lexington's* preliminary combat report listed no damage to mount 2. *National Archives via Rob Stern*

In the foreground, facing aft, is 5-inch mount number 4 in the forward port gallery. Next to the mount is a crewman wearing a life jacket, apparently surveying the damage. The bomb that caused this damage is thought to have weighed less than 200 pounds. *National Archives via Rob Stern*

In a view taken from next to the island, facing forward, around 1700 hours on May 8, 1942, crewmen of *Lexington* prepare to abandon ship. That order would be issued at 1707, when all surviving crewmen, around 2,770 in all, would be evacuated to other ships. *Naval History and Heritage Command*

Following a series of internal explosions and fires on the afternoon of May 8, *Lexington's* power plant was shut down at 1630, and at 1707 Capt. Frederick Sherman gave the order to abandon ship. In this photo, crewmen are lowering themselves by lines into the water. *US Naval Shipbuilding Museum*

The abandoning of *Lexington* was well documented in numerous photographs. In this one, crewmen are using knotted lines to hoist themselves up onto one of *Lexington's* escort ships, which did heroic service fighting fires on the carrier and rescuing its crew. *San Diego Air and Space Museum*

At 1727 on May 8, 1942, a large internal explosion amidships, thought to have been caused by the detonation of torpedo warheads, blew off the aft elevator and hurled aircraft into the air. This photograph shows that catastrophic explosion. *Naval History and Heritage Command*

The massive explosion set off by the detonation of ordnance at 1727 is viewed a moment after the preceding photograph was taken. The escort ships had backed away from the carrier by then. More of *Lexington's* crewmen were killed in the explosion. *US Navy*

Following the massive explosion, *Lexington* is a seething mass of destruction amidships. Amazingly, aircraft are still present at the rear of the flight deck. Many crewmen were still on the carrier at this time, attempting to get off the ship. *US Navy*

After a series of explosions wracked *Lexington* in the late afternoon of May 8, the destroyer USS *Phelps* (DD-360) was ordered to sink the mortally wounded carrier. *Phelps* sent three torpedoes into *Lexington*, and the ship went below the waves at 1956. *US Navy*

The sinking of USS *Lexington* marked another in a series of dark days for the United States and its navy following the December 7, 1941, attack on Pearl Harbor. In spring 1942, the US Navy had only a handful of carriers in the Pacific and could ill afford to lose one. Although twenty-six officers and 190 crewmen of *Lexington* were lost on May 8, 1942, the balance of her crew, 2,735 in all, was saved, and these officers and men, with the benefit of battle experience, would go on to staff the carriers that soon would flow from America's shipyards to the battle fronts. Lady Lex, as she was affectionately called by her crew, helped hold the line against Japanese expansion in the South Pacific in those perilous first months of the war, and she would stand as a powerful symbol of American resolve. *San Diego Air and Space Museum*

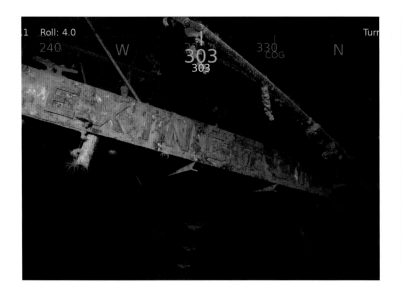

On March 5, 2018, a team assembled by the late Paul G. Allen located the remains of *Lexington* on the floor of the Coral Sea. *Paul G. Allen*

One of the seven TBD Devastator torpedo bombers located in the *Lexington* debris field. These aircraft are among the only known existent examples of the type. *Paul G. Allen*

Among *Lexington's* debris is this VF-3 F4F-3 Wildcat, which was flown by Noel Gaylor. Visible beneath the canopy are four kill markings, as well as the VF-3 "Felix the Cat" logo. *Paul G. Allen*

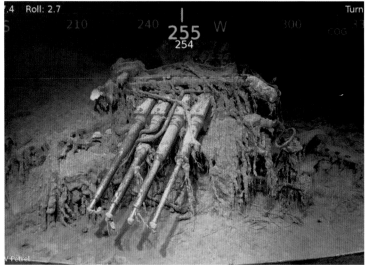

This quadruple 1.1-inch antiaircraft gun was once part of *Lexington's* antiaircraft battery. *Paul G. Allen*